IMAGES
of America

MANHATTAN
HOTELS
1880–1920

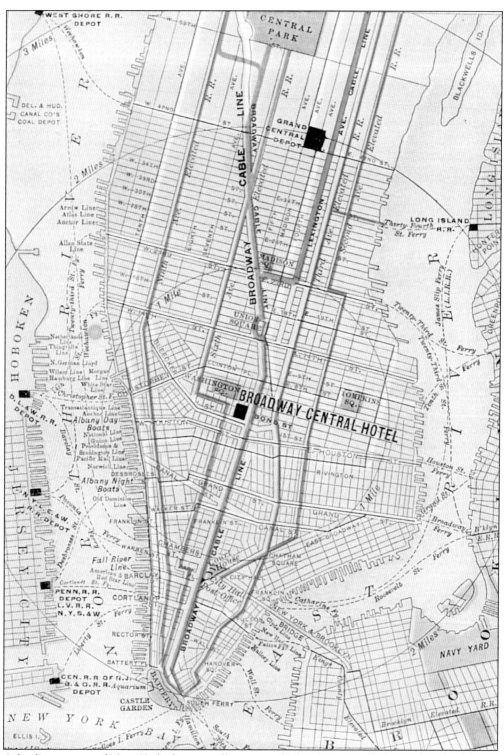

A bird's-eye map of New York showing all steamer docks, ferries, and elevated and cable car lines. Issued by the Broadway Central Hotel in the early 1890s.

IMAGES
of America

MANHATTAN HOTELS 1880–1920

Jeff Hirsh

ARCADIA
PUBLISHING

Copyright © 1997 by Jeff Hirsh
ISBN 978-0-7385-5749-6

Published by Arcadia Publishing
Charleston, South Carolina

Printed in the United States of America

Library of Congress Catalog Card Number: 2007940443

For all general information contact Arcadia Publishing at:
Telephone 843-853-2070
Fax 843-853-0044
E-mail sales@arcadiapublishing.com
For customer service and orders:
Toll-Free 1-888-313-2665

Visit us on the Internet at www.arcadiapublishing.com

The Broadway Central Hotel, Broadway and the corner of Third Street, from an 1890s engraving. The trolleys running past the hotel are Broadway Line cable cars.

Contents

Broadway at Astor Square. The Astor House hotel is on the left.

Acknowledgments

My thanks to the many generous individuals who made this book possible with their suggestions and by sharing information and images with me. In particular I am indebted to the library staff of the New-York Historical Society, my friends Dorothy and Carlton Bloodgood, and Edward B. Epstein, Garth Davidson of Garth Davidson Gallery, David Bard of the Chelsea Hotel, the St. Regis Hotel, and the extensive image archives of Roslyn Manor Antique Postcards on Greeting Cards.

Hotels Netherlands and Savoy facing Central Park and the Plaza Hotel. They are seen here as they appeared just after the turn of the century.

Introduction

By 1880, the whole nature of hotels and the hotel experience were undergoing dramatic changes. Hotels were no longer merely a place to stop on the road between here and there for a hot meal and a warm bed.

Now the hotel, itself, was becoming the destination.

Many of those things we now take for granted in modern hotels were introduced or became expected in this period. Bursts of exciting new technology, spreading affluence and changing fashion all came together in the decades between 1880 and 1920 to alter hotels beyond recognition and vastly increase the demands and expectations of their guests.

Manhattan almost always magnifies and exaggerates trends. This was most certainly the case as the city's hotels struggled mightily to keep pace with the demands of a town exploding into a modern metropolis. The soaring value of Manhattan real estate mandated that hotels upend their basic horizontal layout and turn themselves into vertical boxes. Two exciting new technologies made this possible.

First the elevator came of age. Primitive steam driven models were superceded by faster, more efficient and reliable lifts powered by electric motors.

New buildings with steel girder skeletons and curtain walls began to replace older structures that depended on load bearing walls. This took the lid off height limitations, unleashing the modern skyscraper hotel.

In this period, too, hotels replaced old fashioned gas lighting with electric lights. The telephone made it possible to reserve rooms on short notice and even call down from your room for service. When the new Plaza opened just after the turn of the century, the hotel proudly advertised a phone in every room.

As the middle class multiplied and affluence spread, a new mass market blossomed for luxurious hotel accommodations. This was fueled by growing numbers of travellers embarking or returning from an ocean voyage. Steamships were becoming floating luxury hotels, and patrons expected nothing less from their land-based counterparts.

The vast influx of immigrants in this period provided Manhattan hotels with an abundance of low wage service workers. Some luxury hotels maintained a staff to guest ratio of one to one or even higher as they sought to deliver superb service night and day.

In 1903, the St. Regis pioneered central air conditioning with individual controls in every room. On a more mundane level, a room with private bath evolved from a rare luxury into a standard feature.

The look of hotels changed radically between 1880 and 1920. In 1880, the style was unmistakably Victorian. By the mid-1890s, the fashion was moving to a more reserved Edwardian elegance. Around 1912 and continuing through the rest of the decade, the emphasis shifted, first to modern functionalism and by the end to art deco.

No story of Manhattan hotels would be complete without a word or two about the Astors, the clan that dominated the hotel industry all through the nineteenth century and well into the twentieth.

The foundation for the Astor hotel empire was laid by John Jacob Astor. At the beginning of the nineteenth century he recognized that practically the entire population of Manhattan was clustered at the southern tip of the rock.

Astor's vision was that one day Manhattanites would spread out and cover the entire island, and that he would own much of the land in the path of their northward migration. He bought up every square inch he could lay hands on, accumulating vast tracts that included the site on which the Empire State Building now stands, most of Times Square, and countless choice bits and pieces.

Beginning with the Astor House Hotel in 1836, the Astors and their trust managers built one notable hotel after another, including the Waldorf-Astoria, St. Regis, Astor, and the Knickerbocker.

This book is organized as a section-by-section walking tour of hotels operating in Manhattan between 1880 and the 1920s. Illustrations are included from both the earlier and later decades, providing a picture of the changing face of the city and its hotels.

Obviously a book of this size cannot possibly cover every hotel that operated in Manhattan over a span of four decades. This one depicts a broad cross section, ranging from the most fashionable to some down and out "flea bags."

The Vanderbilt mansion and the old Plaza Hotel as it appeared shortly before it was demolished.

A 1905 motorized bus. Within a few years after the turn of the century, tourists were seeing New York aboard motorized buses. This one left from the recently built Flat Iron Building.

The New Netherlands hotel seen from the lake in Central Park.

One

The Fifties

Beginning in the 1880s, a number of the "crown jewels" of Manhattan hotels went up along Fifth Avenue in the fifties. These elegant new establishments would speed the demise of the residential character of the neighborhood. Once the exclusive bedroom suburb of the Vanderbilts and their set, Fifth Avenue was soon beset by noisy traffic and the much feared onset of creeping commercialism. In the early 1890s, Caroline Schermerhorn Astor, her son John Jacob Astor IV, and his wife, rejected a site at the southeast corner of 55th Street for their new mansion. A decade later, the vacant lot would hold the newly opened St. Regis Hotel.

(Left) Fifth Avenue. For just a few years after the turn of the century, Fifth Avenue between 50th and 59th Streets was able to maintain its quiet residential character. (Right) By 1905, the motor car and "creeping commercialism" had changed everything.

11

PLAZA HOTEL. 5ᵀᴴ AVENUE, 58ᵀᴴ & 59ᵀᴴ STREETS.
NEW YORK

The Plaza Hotel. Work on the original Plaza Hotel began in 1883 using plans drawn up by architect George W. DeCunha. The builders ran out of money prior to completion. In 1888, New York Life foreclosed and brought in McKim, Mead, and White to redesign the interior. The eight story, 400 room Plaza opened in the fall of 1890 and is depicted here in an 1893 trade card. The demise of the "old" Plaza was decreed at the St. Regis one afternoon over lunch. The owners of the Plaza, Harry A. Black, president of Fuller Construction Company, and Bernhard Beinecke, a wholesale butcher, were discussing how to earn a return on their $3 million investment. The old hotel had too few rooms to generate sufficient cash flow. Adding floors was no option, the load bearing walls would not carry the weight. John Gates, a speculator, overheard the conversation. He offered financial backing for building a "new" Plaza, and the deal was made over lunch.

The "new" Plaza Hotel. New York architect, Henry J. Hardenbergh, was retained to design the "new" Plaza Hotel. He opted for the new steel skeleton technology that had been used earlier by Harry Black, the hotel's co-owner, when he built the Flat Iron Building. The eighteen-story brick and marble French Renaissance-style Plaza Hotel cost over $12.5 million. The hotel had eight hundred rooms and five hundred baths when it opened in the fall of 1907. It had centrally controlled electric clocks and telephones in every room. The public area had crystal chandeliers, marble fireplaces and staircases, and no end of elegant appointments.

Two near neighbors of the Plaza. (*Left*) The Astor family began assembling the site of the New Netherland hotel in the years following the Civil War. The hotel stood on the northeast corner of 59th Street and Fifth Avenue. (*Below*) The Savoy was designed by Ralph Townsend. It was built in 1892 on the southeast corner of 59th Street and Fifth Avenue.

Interiors of the Hotel Netherland. (*Above*) The Empire Room. (*Below*) The Dutch Room.

(*Above*) A Maxfield Parish triptych. *Old King Cole and His Fiddlers Three*, long a landmark at the St. Regis, was originally commissioned for the Knickerbocker Hotel. (*Below*) The elegant Louis XVI bedroom at the St. Regis as it appeared in 1915.

The St. Regis Hotel. Colonel John Jacob Astor, author of a science fiction novel and devotee of such curiosities as the flying machine and turbine engine, was convinced the steel frame technology that made skyscraper office towers possible was equally valid for hotels. In 1901 he commissioned Trowbridge & Livingston to put his theories to test. They designed the St. Regis, then the city's tallest hotel and one of its most fashionable. Its daring innovations included a central vacuum system, and automatic thermostats that let guests select heated, dried, moistened or cooled air.

(*Left*) The Great Northern fronted on West 56th and 57th Streets. For a time it was owned by heavyweight champion and restaurateur Jack Dempsey. (*Below*) The elegant marble foyer of the Great Northern Hotel.

The Gotham. This hotel has the dubious distinction of being the only fashionable turn-of-the-century New York City hotel to go belly up. Architects Hiss & Weekes were retained to draw up plans for the eighteen-story hotel by a consortium of speculators led by Senators Thomas Forturne Ryan and Mark A. Hanna. By opening day in 1905, management knew it was in deep trouble. The hotel's close proximity to St. Lukes made it impossible to obtain a liquor license.

Hotel Cumberland, 54th Street and Broadway.

(*Right*) The Hotel Woodward at Broadway and 55th Street. (*Below*) Hotel Commonwealth, a real estate venture that collapsed just after 1920, before the hotel could be built. It was slated to occupy the entire square block bordered by Broadway, 55th and 56th Streets and Seventh Avenue. The 2,500-room hotel would have been the largest in the world.

Hotel Albemarle, on 54th Street near Broadway.

The Ambassador Hotel, New York City.

The Ambassador Hotel on Park Avenue between 51st and 52nd Streets. The Ambassador quickly became a fashionable rendezvous in the post war era.

Ritz Tower Building,
Park Ave. and 57th St.,
New York City.

The Ritz Tower, Park Avenue and 57th Street, built in 1926.

Two

The East Forties

The focal point for hotel action in the East Forties was Grand Central Depot. It was designed by John B. Snook, and completed in 1871. By the 1890s, the station was hopelessly inadequate for its traffic volume. As a stopgap measure, a new and larger baroque structure was grafted onto the original station. Grand Central Depot was demolished in 1913 to make way for a large new structure that became the focal point of the Vanderbilt Terminal City development. Seven hotels were included in the plan, not all of which were built.

(*Left*) The baroque structure grafted onto Grand Central Depot in the 1890s. (*Right*) The new Grand Central Terminal completed in 1913.

(Above) The Grand Union Hotel. The Grand Union's mansard roof and Second Empire styling clearly reflected the look of Grand Central Depot, located just across the street from the hotel. The Grand Union Hotel opened in 1874 to cater to the growing number of visitors arriving by train. *(Below)* The Grand Union Hotel as it appeared just a few years before it was demolished in 1914 to make way for subway construction.

The Hotel Manhattan. A decade before he designed the "new" Plaza Hotel, architect Henry J. Hardenbergh designed the elegant fourteen-story Hotel Manhattan. Located on the west side of Madison Avenue between 42nd and 43rd Streets, Hotel Manhattan opened in 1896. Its stylish Italian Renaissance façade was of Indiana limestone, with columns of Green Island granite. Inside there was a Tiffany "Favrille" glass mosaic.

(*Above*) An elegant private suite at the Murray Hill Hotel. (*Below*) Ladies writing room, reading room, and library at the Murray Hill Hotel.

Murray Hill Hotel, NEW YORK.

WORLD'S FAIR SOUVENIR.
SPECIMEN OF COLOR PRINTING.

J. Ottmann Lith. Co.
PUCK BUILDING,
NEW YORK

GRAND CENTRAL STATION

OVER

(*Above*) The Murray Hill Hotel. The hotel was designed by architect, Stephen Hatch. The eight-story, six hundred-room gem of a hotel opened in 1884. It was situated on Park Avenue between 40th and 41st Streets. The brownstone, granite and brick façade was flanked by two ornamental towers. The hotel's public rooms had red and white marble floors and rococo decor. Among the noted celebrities who stayed at the Murray Hill were Mark Twain, Jay Gould, Diamond Jim Bradey, and Presidents Grover Cleveland and William McKinley. The Murray Hill was demolished at the end of the Second World War and replaced by an office building. (*Below*) The lobby of the Murray Hill Hotel.

Italian Garden, The Biltmore Hotel, New York

The Biltmore Hotel's Italian Garden as it appeared in 1914.

The Biltmore Hotel. The Biltmore was designed by architects Warren and Wetmore in an innovative "H" plan that gave outside exposure to every one of its 1,000 rooms. When it was built in 1913 by the New York Central Railroad, it was conceived as part of the grand plan for Terminal City, a complex of seven hotels. It was linked below ground to adjacent Grand Central Terminal. The brick and terra-cotta facade is in a modernized Italian Renaissance style.

(*Above*) The Hotel Commodore. This hotel boasted of having the world's most beautiful lobby. (*Below*) The Commodore's Century Room was played by many of America's most famous dance bands.

The Hotel Commodore, designed by the firm of Warren and Wetmore, the prolific architects responsible for the Ritz Carlton, Vanderbilt, and Biltmore. Opened in December 1917, the hotel had 2,000 rooms, all of them with baths and circulating ice water. The Commodore exemplified the shift from Edwardian elegance to functional modern.

Hotel Belmont, New York.

Hotel Belmont, 42nd Street and Park Avenue. The twenty-three-floor, 750-room hotel was designed by New York architects Warren & Wetmore and opened in 1906. It was demolished in 1931.

Three

The West Forties

As theaters and clubs moved uptown into the west forties, hotels followed rapidly in their wake. At the turn of the century, the area was known as Long Acre Square. It was renamed Times Square just a few years later with the opening of the Times Building.

(*Left*) Broadway looking north to Times Square. (*Right*) The Hippodrome Theatre, 6th Avenue between 43rd and 44th, was just one of the many theaters built in or near Times Square.

Hotel Astor on the left, looking north up Broadway and Seventh Avenue. The photograph was taken circa 1905 from the top of the Times Building.

The French Renaissance-style, 700-room Astor Hotel. The Astor was built in 1903 by William Waldorf Astor on Long Acre Square, soon to be renamed Times Square. In 1907 the Astor was the site of treaty negotiations between Andrew Carnegie and representatives of the Japanese government. Nine years later, candidate Charles Evans Hughes would go to bed at the Astor believing he had won the presidency. Hughes awoke the next morning to learn that his failure to carry California had cost him the election, giving Woodrow Wilson his second term. General George Pershing stayed at the Astor the night before he left for Europe to command the American Expeditionary Forces. Over the years, nine presidents were among the Astor's 15 million guests.

Some of New York's finest hotels maintained staff-to-guest ratios of 1:1, and occasionally even higher, in an effort to provide superb round-the-clock service. *(Top)* The Astor Hotel's vast kitchen; *(Center)* the wine vaults; *(Bottom)* The Indian Grill Room.

The Astor was one of Manhattan's most fashionable night spots. *(Top)* The Belvedere. *(Bottom)* The Orangerie.

The Pabst Hotel. The eight-story Pabst was one of the first hotels to make use of the new steel frame technology. It was built in 1899 in Long Acre Square on the triangle of land between 42nd and 43rd Streets. Designed by Henry F. Kilburn, the hotel was leased to the Pabst Brewing Company and quickly became profitable. Unfortunately, its rathskeller stood squarely in the path of the projected uptown extension of the Interborough Rapid Transit subway. A deal was struck in 1902 whereby the hotel was to be demolished and replaced by the Times Building. Each of the thousands of rivet heads in its steel frame had to be individually cut off in order to disassemble the skeleton.

The Knickerbocker Hotel. In 1906, Colonel John Jacob Astor commissioned architects Marvin & Davis and later Trowbridge & Livingston to design The Knickerbocker at Broadway and 42nd Street. The hotel would provide Fifth Avenue luxuries at Broadway prices. A single room cost just $2 a day; a three-room, two bath suite went for $20. Colonel Astor was right on target with his selection of the location. There were twenty-eight theaters within a five-block radius, the Met was down the block, and the hotel soon became a favorite haunt of Enrico Caruso.

A 1908 photograph of the large kitchen staff of the Knickerbocker.

Interiors at the fashionable Knickerbocker Hotel. *(Top)* The cafe. *(Bottom)* The banquet hall.

(Left) Commodore Club Hotel, 351 West 42nd Street. *(Right)* Hotel Continental, Broadway and 41st Street.

(Right) Hotel Wallick, Broadway and 43rd Street. *(Below)* West Shore Hotel at the corner of 11th Avenue and 42nd Street as it appeared around 1908. The hotel was demolished in 1936.

WEST SHORE HOTEL 11TH AVE. & 42ND ST. NEW YORK CITY

(*Above*) Dining room of the Hotel Woodstock. (*Below*) The hotel's lounge.

The Langwell Hotel, 123–129 West 44th Street.

(*Left*) Hotel Woodstock, 127–135 West 43rd Street. (*Below*) Hotel Cadillac, Broadway and 43rd Street.

(Right) Hotel Claridge, Broadway and 44th Street. *(Below)* The lobby of the Claridge.

(*Above*) The lounge at Hotel Piccadilly. (*Below*) The main restaurant.

Hotel Piccadilly, 227 West 45th Street.

The Algonquin Hotel. H.L. Mencken called The Algonquin "The most comfortable hotel in America." No matter, the hotel will always be best known for the urbane wit of the literary crowd that daily held forth at its infamous round table. Among them were Dorothy Parker, Robert Benchley, Edna Ferber and Alexander Wolcott. When the Algonquin opened in 1902, it was called The Puritan. The renting agent, Frank Case, became obsessed with the idea that the name was cold and forbidding. He went to the New York Public Library to determine the name of the neighborhood's "first and strongest people." They turned out to be the Algonquin and the hotel was renamed.

Hotel Richmond, 70–72 West 46th Street, in a photograph taken around 1910.

The French Renaissance-style Hotel Paramount on 46th Street just west of Broadway. All of the hotel's 700 rooms had private baths and were served with ice water. The hotel's grill was a popular dining and dancing spot in the post war era.

(*Right*) Hotel Flanders, 133–137 West 47th Street, in a photograph taken around 1905. (*Below*) Hotel Somerset, 150 West 47th Street.

Some hotels went through several name changes over the years as they passed from management to management. *(Left)* The Hotel Longacre, Broadway and 47th Street. Opened in November, 1904, the ten-story Longacre was a bachelor hotel that offered such amenities as electric elevators, mail chutes and a filtered water supply. *(Below)* The same hotel in the 1920s, now the Hotel America catering to a mainly Latin clientele.

ONE BLOCK EAST OF BROADWAY,
IN THE VERY CENTRE OF THE THEATRES,
WITHIN EASY WALKING DISTANCE
OF ALL SHOPS, AND CONVENIENT
TO ALL LINES OF TRANSPORTATION

HOTEL BRISTOL
122-124 WEST 49TH STREET
NEW YORK

ROOMS WITH RUNNING WATER, $1.00 PER DAY UP
ROOMS WITH PRIVATE BATH, $2.00 PER DAY UP
SUITES, $5.00 PER DAY UP
AMERICAN PLAN $2.50 PER DAY U

(*Above*) Hotel Bristol, 122–124 West 49th Street, as the block looked around 1910. (*Below*) The Hotel Bristol's dining room.

Hotel Van Cortlandt, 142–146 West 49th Street.

Four

The East Thirties

In 1826, William Backhouse Astor bought a large tract of land in twhat is now the east and west thirties from John Thompson. The parcel ran crosstown from Madison Avenue to Sixth Avenue and north and south between 32nd and 36th Streets. Caroline Schermerhorn Astor had her famous mansion on the corner of 34th Street and Fifth Avenue. The concept of "The Four Hundred" in New York society stems from the fact that the ballroom of her mansion could accommodate just 400 guests. Her ballroom, along with the mansion, were replaced by the Waldorf-Astoria.

(*Left*) Fifth Avenue at the turn of the Century. The Waldorf-Astoria Hotel is on the left. (*Right*) The J.P. Morgan residence and art gallery on Park Avenue.

An evening concert in the main foyer at the Waldorf-Astoria.

The Waldorf-Astoria. The hyphenated Waldorf-Astoria was actually two interconnected Astor family hotels. Both were the work of New York architect, Henry J. Hardenbergh, who designed them in the German Renaissance style. The twelve-story Waldorf was built in 1893 by William Waldorf Astor. It was soon dwarfed and enfolded by the adjacent L-shaped sixteen-story Astoria, built by William's cousin, the former Caroline Schermerhorn. The hotels were joined in 1897. A nasty, long-running fight between Caroline and William led her to instruct Hardenbergh to design the Astoria so that it could be sealed off from the Waldorf at each floor. In the fall of 1929, the Waldorf-Astoria was demolished and the hotel moved to a more fashionable uptown location. The Empire State Building now stands on the original 34th Street and Fifth Avenue site.

(*Above*) The roof garden at the Waldorf-Astoria. (*Below*) The grand ball room arranged for a large banquet.

The Park Avenue Hotel. A. T. Stewart's Hotel for Working Women opened on April 3, 1878. The original idea was to provide permanent housing for the city's working women, as well as hotel services for female visitors. Too expensive for the working women it was to serve, the establishment was relaunched as the Park Avenue Hotel just two months later. It was advertised on this early tradecard "for transient visitors and families desiring the quietude of an elegant home; contiguous to the most fashionable thoroughfares and with means of quick conveyance to all business centers." It claimed to be "absolutely the only fire-proof hotel building in the United States." Despite this, it was badly damaged by fire in 1881 and again in 1902.

The Park Avenue Hotel as it appeared around 1915.

(*Top*) The sunken palm garden as seen from the dining veranda at the Park Avenue Hotel. (*Center*) The dining veranda overlooking the sunken palm garden. (*Bottom*) The grand staircase and lobby.

The 350-room, ten-story Holland House. The Holland House was built in 1898 on the Southwest corner of Fifth Avenue and 30th Street. The firm of Harding & Gooch designed the hotel in a modified Italian Renaissance style.

Hotel St. Louis, 34–36 East 32nd Street.

Hotel Wolcott, 31st Street off Fifth Avenue.

Five

The West Thirties

With the arrival of numerous large retailers in the area and the opening of Penn Station, hotels soon began to proliferate on the streets around Herald Square. In the decade after the turn of the century, some of the city's largest hotels, such as the Vanderbilt, McAlpin, and Pennsylvania were built in the area.

(*Left*) Broadway looking north from 38th Street. (*Right*) Manhattan Opera House on West 34th Street.

The Louis XVI Grand Salon at the Hotel Imperial as it appeared at the turn of the century.

The seventeen-story Hotel Imperial, Broadway between 31st and 32nd Streets, was designed by the noted New York architects McKim, Meade & White. It was built in 1890 and demolished in 1947.

The Grand Hotel, also known as the Manger Grand Hotel, located at Broadway and 31st Street. The Grand Hotel was close to Macys, Gimbels, and several other large retailers. It offered inexpensive rooms for commercial travellers and maintained "50 large, light sample rooms" for their use.

(*Above*) The ornate dining room of the Martinique was once among the city's most glamorous meeting spots. Conditions gradually deteriorated. By the 1980s, the Martinique was temporary housing for the homeless. (*Below*) The 600-room French Renaissance style Hotel Martinique. The hotel, located on Broadway between 32nd and 33rd Streets, was built in 1897. It was designed by Henry J. Hardenbergh.

(Left) The Herald Square Hotel, 34th Street just west of Broadway. *(Below)* Hotel Gregorian, 35th Street between Broadway and Fifth Avenue.

(Above) The Hotel Marlborough. This hotel was built in 1888, and was located at 36th Street just west of Broadway. *(Below)* Architects Barney & Chapman designed the 400-room Navarre Hotel, Seventh Avenue at 38th Street. It opened in 1890 and was demolished in 1925.

Hotel Vanderbilt, New York.

The Vanderbilt Hotel. One of the earliest hotels to lead the shift from Edwardian styling to the modern look was the Vanderbilt, which opened in January, 1912. Alfred Gwynne Vanderbilt retained Warren and Wetmore to design the hotel, situated at Park Avenue and 34th Street, on land he inherited from his father.

The McAlpin Hotel on Herald Square.

The roof garden of the Hotel Pennsylvania.

The formal dining room.

Hotel Pennsylvania, New York City.

The Hotel Pennsylvania. When the hotel opened in 1919 on the west side of Seventh Avenue between 32nd and 33rd Streets near Pennsylvania Station, it was the largest hotel in the world. The establishment had 2,200 rooms, all with baths. Hotel Pennsylvania was designed by the firm of McKim, Mead and White. In much the same vein as its contemporaries near Grand Central, the hotel heralded the swing to modern functionalism and the end of Edwardian elegance at the close of World War One.

Six

The Twenties

Madison Square was an important center for hotels long before architect Stanford White turned it into a showplace with his flamboyant Madison Square Garden. White's Moorish masterpiece replaced a dilapidated old train shed long used by Phineas T. Barnum for circus performances.

The square was conveniently close to the northern tip of the fashionable "Ladies Mile," an elegant shopping area strung out along Broadway. In the 1880s, the square was also an easy walk from much of the city's commercial action.

(Left) Madison Square Garden's 300-foot-high tower took its inspiration from Seville's twelfth-century Moorish Giralda Tower. *(Right)* The 1902 Flat Iron Building was one of the early skyscrapers built with the new steel beam technology.

The Chelsea, one of Manhattan's first co-ops. When it opened in 1884, the forty-unit apartment building was the tallest building in town. It was designed by Hubert Pirsson & Company in an American Gothic style tinged with a melange of French and English details. In 1905, the Chelsea was converted into a hotel, and has always been home to artists, writers and assorted creative types. To this day, the Chelsea is more a New York happening than a Victorian artifact. Exciting creative ideas have always poured profusely from the Chelsea. Their roots go back to such guests as Mark Twain, O. Henry, and Sarah Bernhardt. More recently, photos for Madonna's book, *Sex,* were shot at the hotel, as were scenes from movies by Andy Warhol and Woody Allen. Arthur Miller wrote *After the fall* and *Incident at Vichy.* Thomas Wolfe wrote *You can't go home again.* Virgil Thompson composed an opera. Larry Rivers and André François painted there. The list continues to lengthen with each passing decade.

(Right) Twisting tendrils of wrought iron grace the ornate staircase at the Chelsea. *(Below)* A ceiling painted in 1883 by an unknown Italian artist during the construction of the Chelsea bears a striking resemblance to those in some of the Newport mansions.

(*Above*) Madison Cottage, a stagecoach stop and inn. This inn stood on the corner of Broadway and 23rd Street, the site later occupied by the Fifth Avenue Hotel. (*Below*) The six-story Fifth Avenue Hotel was far ahead of its time when developer Amos Eno built it between 1856 and 1858. It was the first hotel in the city with elevators. They were steam driven and were commonly referred to as the "vertical steam engine." There were fireplaces in every bedroom and private bathrooms.

(*Above*) The Fifth Avenue Hotel. With a staff of 400 to care for up to 800 guests, the hotel had a reputation for providing some of the finest service in the city. For a number of years it was headquarters of the state Republican Party. (*Below*) Madison Square gradually became less fashionable as the trade moved north. The Ladies Mile, Broadway's premier shopping corridor, also deteriorated. In 1908 the ageing Fifth Avenue Hotel was demolished and replaced with the Fifth Avenue Building.

(*Left*) Hotel Victoria at the corner of Broadway and 27th Street. (*Below*) Construction began in 1903 on the twelve-story, 176 room Broztell Hotel. Located at Fifth Avenue and 27th Street in the heart of the theater and club district, the new hotel offered a room with private bath and shower for one person for $1.50. Architect H.B. Birkmire designed a distinctive entrance for the Broztell, featuring handsome doors of wrought iron and glass.

Hotel Aldine, Fourth Avenue between 29th and 30th Streets. Despite its modest appearance, every room in this seven-story hotel came with a private bath.

The hotels of Madison Square. In the opening decade of the twentieth century, five stately hotels—the Prince George, Seville, Martha Washington, Madison Square, and Arlington—went up in the neighborhood surrounding Madison Square. The most prominent of the group was the Prince George. (*Left*) The main hall and 27th Street entrance. (*Below*) The formal dining room.

PRINCE GEORGE HOTEL, NEW YORK

At the St. George. (*Top*) The Tea Room. (*Center*) The English Tap Room. (*Bottom*) The Italian Room.

(*Left*) The Martha Washington Hotel. The Martha Washington served women guests exclusively, was located at 29 East 29Th Street. (*Below*) The lobby of the Martha Washington.

(*Above*) The Madison Square Hotel. The Madison stood on the east side of Madison Square at 37 Madison Avenue. (*Below*) Hotel Seville, Fifth Avenue and 29th Street.

The venerable Hoffman House, at Broadway and Madison Square. The Hoffman House was designed by Reed, Wall & Company and opened in 1864, The hotel was the scene of many Democratic Party victory celebrations. It was demolished in 1915 and replaced by an office building.

The Arlington Hotel on 25th Street near Broadway and Fifth.

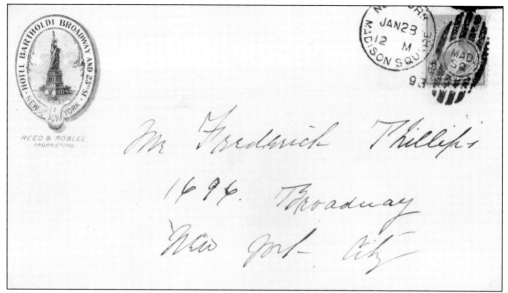

Mr Frederick Phillips
1694. Broadway
New York City

(*Above*) Hotel Bartholdi was an 8-story hotel built in 1885 and named for the sculptor of the Statue of Liberty. The structure was converted to commercial purposes in 1926 and was demolished in 1970. (*Below*) The twelve-story Breslin Hotel on the Southeast corner of Broadway & 29th Street. The hotel was built in 1902 by the Fuller Construction Company, the firm that built the Flat Iron Building. The Breslin replaced the Sturtevant House, a hotel that had stood on the site since 1878

Seven

Lower Manhattan

By the turn of the century, many lower Manhattan neighborhoods from the Battery to 14th Street were losing their luster as centers for fashionable hotels.

An exception was Washington Square in Greenwich Village, which continued as a desirable location even as nearby areas were slipping into decline.

(*Left*) Washington Square looking into Fifth Avenue. (*Right*) Trolleys enter Manhattan from the Brooklyn Bridge.

(Left) The Abingdon Hotel. The Abingdon was located on 8th Avenue near 12th Street, and overlooked Abingdon Square, not far from many of the Hudson River piers. The hotel advertised itself as "Best located for European travellers." It offered to send its representatives to meet passengers at any steamship pier. (Below) The Hotel Churchill on Union Square, Broadway and 14th Street, seen here as it appeared around 1915.

(Above) Astor House. This was the first of countless hotels built by members of the Astor family in the city. It opened in 1836. *(Below)* One of the few Manhattan hotels to survive in the business for one hundred years, the Brevoort , Fifth Avenue and Eighth Street, was built in 1854. President Garfield, Mark Twain, Isadora Duncan, Count Leo Tolstoi, Theodore Dreiser and Eugene O'Neill were just a few of the well known individuals who stayed at the Brevoort. The hotel was demolished in 1954 and replaced by an apartment complex.

The twelve-story Hotel Albert. The Albert was built around 1903 at the Southeast corner of University Place and 11th Street. Over the years, the Hotel went through many alterations and the addition of various annexes. *(Left)* Hotel Albert as it appeared around 1910. *(Below)* The new Hotel Albert, after a facelift and extensive rebuilding.

The Hotel Lafayette. The hotel was opened in 1902 by Raymond Orteig, who would later be known for putting up the $25,000 in prize money that Linburgh earned for his solo flight to Paris. The Lafayette and its elegant cafe were frequented by such personalities as the dancer and model Yvette Gilbert, authors Mark Twain, Henry James, and Robert Louis Stevenson, Clemenceau and Wendell Willkie. The building dates back to the 1870s, when it was known as the Pension La Rue and Cafe Martin.

(*Left*) Hotel Earle and (*Below*) Hotel Holley, both on Washington Square, were unusual for Manhattan hotels in the post WW1 era, in that they operated on the American plan.

Hotel Holley,
Washington Square,
New York City.

(*Above*) The ladies' and gentlemen's grill at the St. Denis Hotel. (*Below*) In the 1880s, the St. Denis Hotel, Broadway and 11th Street, was strategically located in the fashionable Ladies Mile shopping district. Directly across the street was James McCreery & Co., one of the city's finer department stores. Over the years, the neighborhood and its shops gradually became less fashionable and the fortunes of the St. Denis declined apace. In 1904, the St. Denis pioneered the switch to central station electrical service, abandoning its own steam plant and electric generating facility.

The Broadway Central. In its time, the Broadway Central was one of New York's finest hotels. The building began its checkered career as Tripler Hall in 1850, completed behind schedule, just slightly too late to house Jenny Lind's New York debut. The Swedish Nightingale did, however give 15 concerts there in the fall of that year. The building was remodeled and reopened in 1869 as the Grand Central Hotel. Robber baron Jim Fisk was ambushed and killed in the lobby in 1872 by Edward Stokes in a quarrel over the affections of actress Jessie Mansfield. In 1892 the hotel was renamed the Broadway Central. The Broadway Central met its end when an overhead crack gave way on August 3, 1973. The hotel collapsed into a giant heap of rubble.

(*Above*) The all-male Puritan Hotel at 183 Bowery. (*Below*) Smith & McNell's Hotel and Dining Room, 198-200 Greenwich Street.

The fifteen-story Libby's Hotel and Baths on Delancey Street, on the lower East Side. The hotel was designed by architects Gronenberg & Leuchtag.

Eight

Central Park and Above

By the mid 1880s, an elevated line and cable cars linked the Upper West Side with the rest of the city. The lure of vast profits to be made from building housing for the city's rapidly growing middle class set off successive waves of real estate speculation and cycles of boom and bust.

   The blocks from Central Park West to the river never had the cachet of their East Side counterparts. Nevertheless, moderate rents and the transformation of Broadway above Columbus Circle into a European style tree-lined boulevard attracted thousands of families to the area.

(Left) Columbus Circle looking north. *(Right)* Pedestrians strolling on Riverside Drive.

Hotel Empire, Broadway & 63rd Street.

The twelve-story Hotel Marie Antoinette, Broadway & 67th Street.

The Majestic Hotel. In 1891, Jacob Rothchild began buying up parkfront lots on Central Park West between 71st and 72nd, generally paying about $25,000 apiece. With the entire frontage under his control, he commissioned Alfred Zucker to design the twelve-story Majestic Hotel. Load bearing walls limited the building's height. Construction costs, originally estimated at a million, were probably about twice that. The inaugural ball was held at the Majestic in December 1894. By 1900, the Majestic was joined along the park by a number of similar establishments, including the San Remo, the Beresford and the Eldorado.

The Ansonia. William Earl Dodge Stokes, a speculator, put up the Ansonia, a major apartment hotel, on the west side of Broadway between 73rd and 74th Streets. Stokes worked closely with architect Paul Duboy on the design of the $7 million, sixteen-story Ansonia, an overblown Belle Epoque affair.

The Hotel Belleclaire, Broadway and 77th Street. The Belleclaire is one of just a handful of Manhattan buildings in the Art Nouveau style. Emery Roth designed the hotel in 1900, and it fit in perfectly with the neighborhood's air of European elegance. Shortly after the Belleclaire opened in 1903, it was involved in a minor scandal. Russian Socialist Maxim Gorky, on a lecture tour, registered there with a companion who he claimed was his wife. The lady turned out to be the Russian actress Madame Andreieva. The Belleclaire's manager ejected Gorky, stating that his was a family hotel. The incident made all of the city's newspapers and several hotels refused to provide rooms for the party.

Manhattan Square Hotel, 50–58 West 77th Street.

The public lounge of the Hotel Endicott, Columbus Avenue & 81st street. The Endicott, built in 1889, was one of the oldest hotels on the upper west side. The architect was Edward L. Angell.

(Right) The 300-room Hotel Lucerne, 201 West 79th Street. (Below) Bretton Hall Hotel, Broadway between 85th & 86th Streets.

(*Left*) The twenty-three-story, 1,000 room Hotel Paris, West End Avenue at 97th Street, a late comer on the upper west side scene, was designed by architect H. Hurwitt. (*Below*) The ten-story Hotel Marseilles, Broadway at 103rd Street, was known for the splendid views from its roof garden.

King's Crown Hotel, 420 West 116th Street.

The Hotel Theresa. When it opened in 1913, the thirteen-story Theresa was the tallest building in Harlem. The handsome white brick and terra cotta hotel was designed by George and Edward Blum. Situated at 125th Street and Broadway, one of the busiest spots in Harlem, the hotel did not serve blacks until 1937, when it was acquired by a prominent black businessman. The Theresa's penthouse dining room featured stunning views of the Palisades and Long Island Sound. It was for many years a favorite uptown night spot.

(*Above*) The historic Claremont Hotel, located near Grant's tomb on a bluff overlooking the Hudson. It was once the residence of Joseph Bonapart who was named King of Spain by Napoleon. (*Below*) The Vanderbilts arriving at the Claremont in their coach.

Ben Riley's Arrowhead Inn, 177th Street and the Hudson River.

Nine

Manhattan on Vacation

With the exception of the switch from horizontal to vertical structures, all of the changes that swept over Manhattan hotels between 1880 and the 1920s are reflected in the nearby out of town hotels.

River and ocean steamers, train lines, and finally the motor car all combined to make these hotels increasingly accessible and attractive as vacation spots for Manhattan residents.

The Fall River Line. This line was just one of a number of steamer lines connecting Manhattan residents with nearby vacation sites.

The Mathewson, Narragansett Pier, Rhode Island.

Hotel Pemberton, Windmill Point, and an accompanying advertisement from the Boston & Hingham Steamboat Company and the Nantasket Beach and Railroad Company promoting the pleasures of ocean bathing.

(Above) International Hotel, Niagara Falls. *(Below)* Grand Union Hotel, Saratoga Springs.

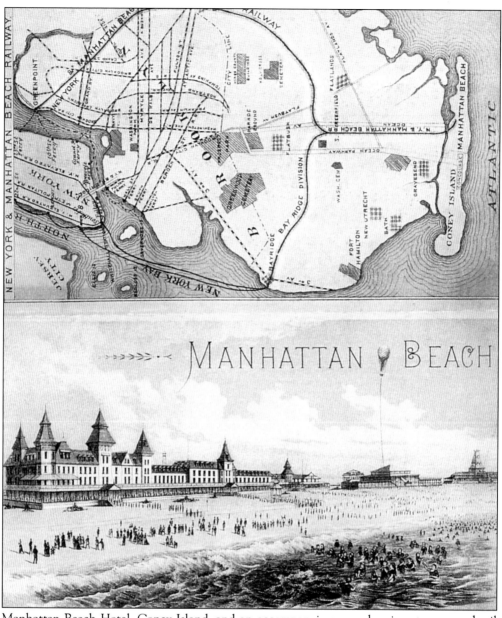

Manhattan Beach Hotel, Coney Island, and an accompanying map showing steamer and rail connections from Manhattan.

(*Above*) Starin's Glen Island Resort on Long Island. (*Below*) Brighton Beach Hotel, Coney Island.

FORT LEE PARK.

Fort Lee Park Hotel and Pavilion on the Hudson, near the present site of the George

FORT LEE ON HUDSON.

DONALDSON BROTHERS, FIVE POINTS,

Washington Bridge.

(*Left*) Hotel Kaaterskill in an 1883 advertisement for the hotel's third season. (*Below*) Sea Beach Palace Hotel, Coney Island.